12/2011

P9-CRC-315

ANCIENT AND MEDIEVAL PEOPLE

The Pharaohs' Armies

Louise Park
and Timothy Love

 **Marshall Cavendish**
Benchmark
New York

This edition first published in 2010 in the United States of America by Marshall Cavendish Benchmark.

Marshall Cavendish Benchmark
99 White Plains Road
Tarrytown, NY 10591
www.marshallcavendish.us

All Internet sites were available and accurate when sent to press.

First published in 2009 by
MACMILLAN EDUCATION AUSTRALIA PTY LTD
15–19 Claremont Street, South Yarra 3141

Visit our website at www.macmillan.com.au or go directly to www.macmillanlibrary.com.au

Associated companies and representatives throughout the world.

Copyright © Louise Park 2009

Library of Congress Cataloging-in-Publication Data

Park, Louise, 1961–
    The pharaohs' armies / by Louise Park and Timothy Love.
       p. cm. – (Ancient and medieval people)
    Includes index.
    ISBN 978-0-7614-4451-0
    1. Armies–Egypt–History–Juvenile literature. 2. Military art and
    science–Egypt–History–Juvenile literature. 3. pharaohs–Juvenile
    literature. 4. Egypt–History–To 332 B.C.–Juvenile literature. 5.
    Egypt–History, Military–Juvenile literature. I. Title.
    U31.P34 2009
    355.00932–dc22

                          2008055781

Edited by Julia Carlomagno
Text and cover design by Cristina Neri, Canary Graphic Design
Page layout by Cristina Neri, Canary Graphic Design
Photo research by Legend Images
Illustrations by Colby Heppéll, Giovanni Caselli, and Paul Konye

Printed in the United States

Acknowledgments
The author and the publisher are grateful to the following for permission to reproduce copyright material:

Front cover photos: Giza pyramids © Jan Rihak/iStockphoto; parchment © Selahattin BAYRAM/ iStockphoto

Photos courtesy of: Background photos throughout: old paper © peter zelei/iStockphoto; mosaic tiles © Hedda Gjerpen/iStockphoto; pharaoh statue © Jan Rihak/iStockphoto; Ashwin Kharidehal Abhirama/123RF, 19; Coo-ee Historical Picture Library, 8, 22, 25, 30; Bridgeman Art Library/Getty Images, 26-7 (bottom); Giovanni Caselli's Universal Library Unlimited, 7, 13, 14, 15, 16 (all), 17 (top left, bottom left and bottom right), 24, 26 (top), 27 (top); © DNY59/iStockphoto, 17 (top right); © Jan Rihak/iStockphoto, 4 (pyramids), 23; Photolibrary © North Wind Picture Archives/Alamy, 18; Photolibrary © North Wind Picture Archives/Alamy; Photolibrary © The Print Collector/Alamy, 20; Photolibrary/Art Media, 12; Photolibrary/JD. Dallet, 28; Photolibrary/The Print Collector, 10; Photolibrary/Christian Jegou/SPL, 29; © nagib/Shutterstock, 21.

1 3 5 6 4 2

Contents

Glossary Words

When a word is printed in **bold**, you can look up its meaning in the Glossary on page 31.

Who Were the Pharaohs' Armies?

The pharaohs' armies were Egypt's standing armies, or armies that existed during times of war and peace. They fought to create and expand an empire during the New Kingdom period of Ancient Egypt.

Ancient Egypt

Ancient Egypt is one of the world's oldest civilizations, dating back to 3100 BCE. It was located in northeastern Africa. Ancient Egypt had ten different periods:

❖ Late Predynastic Period (3100–3050 BCE)
❖ Early Dynastic Period (3050–2686 BCE)
❖ Old Kingdom (2686–2160 BCE)
❖ First Intermediate Period (2160–2040 BCE)
❖ Middle Kingdom (2040–1640 BCE)
❖ Second Intermediate Period (1640–1570 BCE)
❖ New Kingdom (1570–1070 BCE)
❖ Third Intermediate Period (1070–712 BCE)
❖ Late Period (712–332 BCE)
❖ Greco–Roman Period (332 BCE–400 CE)

Ancient Egyptian Timeline

1570–1546 BCE
The Hyksos are conquered by Egypt and the New Kingdom is created

1546–1526 BCE
Pharaoh Amenhotep II carries out successful **military campaigns** in Syria–Palestine and begins to build the Egyptian Empire

1425–1417 BCE
Pharaoh Thutmose IV forms an **alliance** with a group of enemies called the Mitanni

1600 BCE — 1500 BCE — 1400 BCE — 1300 BCE

1525–1512 BCE
Pharaoh Thutmose I leads military campaigns in Nubia and Syria

1504–1450 BCE
Pharaoh Thutmose III extends the Egyptian Empire into Syria

1417–1379 BCE
Egypt's wealth is at its peak and **diplomacy** replaces warfare

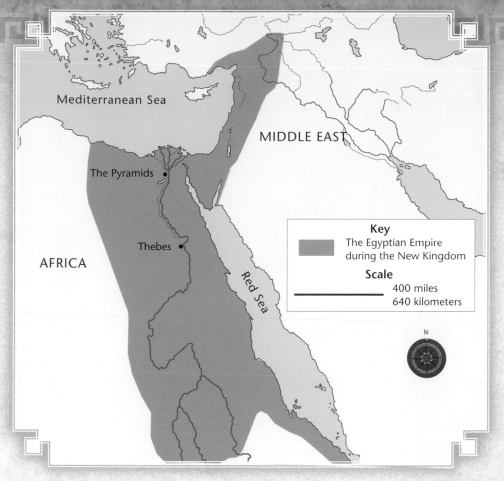

Ancient Egypt's empire extended through northeastern Africa and into the Middle East.

The Development of the Pharaohs' Armies

The pharaohs' armies developed during the First Intermediate Period and the Middle Kingdom. Before this time, Egypt did not have an organized army. Volunteers were called upon to fight for Egypt if it was under attack. Toward the end of the Middle Kingdom, **mercenaries** were hired to serve in the Egyptian army. By the beginning of the New Kingdom, Egypt had formed its first standing army and had begun developing new weapons.

Quick Facts

Who Were Egypt's Enemies?

During the New Kingdom, Egypt had many enemies all over the world.

- ❖ The Hyksos came from Asia.
- ❖ The Hittites once lived in northern Syria.
- ❖ The Sea Peoples were thought to have come from the Eastern Mediterranean.
- ❖ The Mitanni came from northern Mesopotamia.

1318–1304 BCE
Pharaoh Seti I rebuilds the Syria–Palestine part of the empire, which had started to fall away

1236–1223 BCE
Pharaoh Merenptah defeats the Libyans and the Sea Peoples

CE   **1200** BCE   **1100** BCE   **1000** BCE

1304–1237 BCE
Pharaoh Ramses II fights wars against the Hittites

1198–1166 BCE
Pharaoh Ramses III defeats the Libyans and the Sea Peoples

The New Kingdom

The New Kingdom was the seventh period of Ancient Egypt, and it lasted from around 1570 BCE until 1070 BCE. It is often referred to as the Age of Conquest, because during this period Egypt expanded its territories and became a powerful empire.

The Creation of the New Kingdom

Before the New Kingdom, the Hyksos controlled Lower Egypt and the Thebans, from the city of Thebes, controlled Upper Egypt. Ahmose I, the Theban king of Upper Egypt, launched a military campaign against the Hyksos that forced them to retreat to southern Palestine. After years of battle, Lower Egypt finally came under Ahmose I's rule and Egypt was **reunited** as one kingdom. The **expulsion** of the Hyksos and the reunification of Egypt is seen as the beginning of the New Kingdom.

Quick Facts

What Were the Benefits of Hyksos Rule?

The Egyptians gained many new weapons and skills from the Hyksos.

❖ The Hyksos brought new weapons to Egypt, including the chariot and the composite bow. They also preserved many important Egyptian documents, some of which still exist today.

❖ The Thebans learned about warfare from the Hyksos, and this knowledge helped them to drive the Hyksos from Egypt. The pharaohs' armies were based on the Hyksos armies.

Ahmose I drove the Hyksos from Egypt and created what became known as the New Kingdom.

Dynasties of the New Kingdom

Dynasties are periods of time during which one family rules an empire. During the New Kingdom there were three dynasties.

❖ The eighteenth dynasty began around 1550 BCE and ended in 1295 BCE.

❖ The nineteenth dynasty began in 1295 BCE and ended in 1186 BCE.

❖ The twentieth dynasty began in 1186 BCE and ended around 1069 BCE.

During the eighteenth dynasty there were three pharaohs. Ahmose I led from 1570 BCE to 1546 BCE. His son, Amenhotep I, led from 1551 BCE to 1524 BCE. Thutmose I led from 1524 BCE to 1518 BCE.

Building an Empire

The pharaohs of the eighteenth dynasty built an empire around Egypt to ensure that it was too powerful to be invaded again. They achieved this by:

❖ creating **formidable** standing armies

❖ resuming trade with other countries

❖ restoring Egypt's wealth and building up its **treasuries**

❖ constructing **elaborate** temples and tombs

❖ encouraging art, architecture, and culture

WHAT'S IN A NAME?

Ramesside Period

A time known as the Ramesside Period occurred during the nineteenth and twentieth dynasties. The Ramesside Period took its name from the pharaohs who ruled during this time, who were called Ramses. The most famous of these pharaohs was Ramses II.

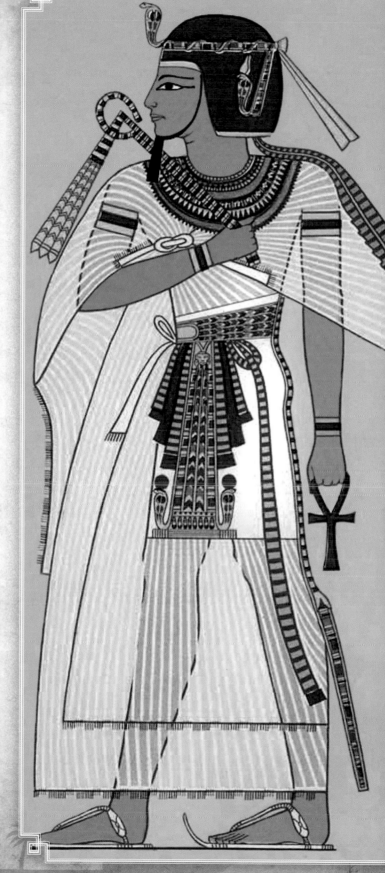

Amenhotep I was one of three pharaohs who ruled during the eighteenth dynasty.

The Role of the Pharaoh

The pharaoh was believed to be the human form of Horus, a powerful Egyptian god. It was the pharaoh's duty to keep order and peace, and to defend Egypt from enemies.

Leading the Egyptian People

The pharaoh was Egypt's religious and political leader, and he led the Egyptian people in a similar manner to a king. He wore a double crown to represent the reunification of Egypt. A red crown represented Lower Egypt and a white crown represented Upper Egypt. The front of the double crown was decorated with a *uraeus*, a rearing cobra which symbolized the Egyptian goddess Wadjet.

Osiris was an Egyptian god believed to have been murdered by his brother, Seth.

Quick Facts

What Was the Legend of Osiris?

The legend of Osiris is an important Egyptian legend that helps to explain the role of the pharaoh.

❖ Osiris was the father of Horus. He was murdered by his brother Seth, the Egyptian god of **chaos**.

❖ The legend tells of how Horus **avenged** the death of his father by defeating Seth.

❖ The battle between Seth and Horus was said to continue endlessly. When Horus won the world was at peace, and when Seth won the world was in chaos. The pharaoh, who was the human form of Horus, was responsible for keeping the world at peace.

Leading the Pharaoh's Army

The pharaoh also led the standing army, which is often known as the pharaoh's army. The pharaoh's army defended Egypt from enemies, and the pharaoh fought in battle alongside his men. In battle, the pharaoh wore a blue crown with a *uraeus* on the front.

Upholding Maat

The pharaoh was expected to uphold Maat for the world. Maat was a set of unspoken laws that promoted truth, balance, order, law, morality, and justice. Egyptians were expected to uphold certain morals and to debate the moral option when faced with a dilemma. Maat was important in the **preservation** of the soul. If the pharaoh went to war, he could persuade the people to support him in order to uphold Maat, protect their souls, and keep the world at peace.

WHAT'S IN A NAME?
Pharaoh
The word *pharaoh* has Greek origins. The Egyptians called the pharaoh *per-aa*, which meant "great house." It originally referred to the palace rather than the ruler.

Egyptian soldiers could recognize the pharaoh in battle because he wore a blue crown.

The Development of the Pharaohs' Armies

After the Hyksos were expelled from Egypt, the pharaohs of the New Kingdom created standing armies to ensure that Egypt was not invaded again. These armies came to be known as the pharaohs' armies.

The Size of the Pharaohs' Armies

The pharaohs' armies consisted of several small divisions, or groups of soldiers. Historians believe that divisions in the pharaohs' armies were each made up of around five thousand soldiers. This meant that they were small enough to travel by ship, which was much faster than marching. As the Egyptian Empire expanded, the need for soldiers increased. The pharaohs' armies began to train prisoners of war as soldiers, in order to boost the size of the armies.

Each division in the pharaohs' armies probably contained around five thousand foot soldiers.

Quick Facts

What Were the Benefits of Being in the Pharaohs' Armies?

Soldiers in the pharaohs' armies were given **social status**, land, and wealth.

❖ Foot soldiers known for their bravery were paid in gold, and sometimes received small parcels of land. Foot soldiers known for their loyalty received daily **provisions** of grains, meat, and wine.

❖ High-ranking officers were given land, which raised their social status. They sometimes shared in treasure and wealth taken from defeated enemies.

❖ Military leaders received prisoners of war to use as slaves. It is believed that Ahmose I once received nineteen slaves after a successful battle.

The pharaoh led the army.

The commander-in-chief reported to the pharaoh and consulted with him on matters of war.

The scribe of infantry reported to the commander-in-chief and kept records of weapons, equipment, and military campaigns.

Foot soldiers fought against Egypt's enemies in battles and military campaigns.

Foot soldiers reported to the nobility, who in turn reported to the pharaoh.

The Hierarchy of the Pharaohs' Armies

The pharaoh's army was led by the pharaoh and the **nobility**, who fought alongside the soldiers. Since the pharaohs' armies were new, they did not have as many traditions and rules as long-standing armies. Therefore, it was easy for a strong and capable solider to rise up through the ranks of the pharaohs' armies. Many soldiers achieved the rank of nobility in this way.

Military Groups

During the New Kingdom, the number of divisions in the pharaoh's armies grew from two to four. Foot soldiers in these divisions were often classified as either infantry soldiers or charioteers.

The Infantry

The infantry, or *mesha*, was the largest group of foot soldiers. It consisted of soldiers who used many different kinds of weapons, including clubs, slings, spears, and arrows. An **elite** group of infantry was known as the Braves of the King. They were the pharaoh's personal guards, and they also led the infantry into battle.

An infantry platoon consisted of around fifty foot soldiers.

Charioteers

Charioteers were the highest-ranking foot soldiers in the pharaohs' armies. They protected infantry soldiers from enemy chariot attacks. Chariots used by the pharaohs' armies were superior to chariots used by other armies around the same period because they were lighter and faster. Each chariot was driven by a soldier who held the reins and a shield. It also carried another soldier who was armed with a composite bow and a spear.

Quick Facts

What Is Known About the Divisions of the Pharaohs' Armies?

The divisions of the pharaohs' armies were named after Egyptian gods, and they grew in number during the New Kingdom.

❖ The four divisions of the pharaohs' armies were named Amun, Ptah, Seth, and Re.

❖ During the eighteenth dynasty, there were only two army divisions. This grew to three during the reign of Seti I and then to four during the reign of Ramses II.

Two charioteers rode in each chariot, which was pulled by a horse.

IN PROFILE: Thutmose I

In Profile

NAME: Thutmose I
TITLE: Pharaoh of Egypt
BORN: Unknown
DIED: 1492 BCE

Thutmose I was a pharaoh of the eighteenth dynasty in the New Kingdom. He is remembered for his military achievements and for establishing the first standing army, or pharaoh's army.

During his reign, Thutmose I fought two key military campaigns, the Nubia campaign and the Syria–Palestine campaign, which led to the conquering of nearby regions Nubia and Syria. By the time of his death Thutmose I had created what would become known as the Egyptian Empire.

Thutmose I's achievements paved the way for the growth of the Egyptian Empire. Several monuments were erected in his name, including pylons (gateways) and **obelisks**.

Notable Moment

During the military campaign against Nubia, Thutmose I ordered that the canal which blocked access between Egypt and Syria be opened. This gave the Egyptians direct access to many places and increased opportunities for trade.

Thutmose I Timeline

1525 BCE **1520 BCE** **1515 BCE**

1526 BCE
Builds a fortress near the canal between Nubia and Egypt to give Egypt a permanent military presence in the area

1525 BCE
Leads a military campaign into Nubia and orders the dredging of the canal

1524 BCE
Becomes pharaoh of Egypt

The Valley of the Kings

Thutmose I was the first pharaoh to be buried in the Valley of the Kings. The valley is located on the west bank of the Nile River in Egypt. For nearly five hundred years, from the 1600s to 1100s BCE, famous pharaohs and members of the nobility were buried there. The Valley of the Kings contains around sixty tombs, stretched across two areas called the East Valley and the West Valley. Most of the royal tombs are in the East Valley.

The tomb of Thutmose I is located in the East Valley of the Valley of Kings.

What You Should Know About...

Thutmose I

❖ Thutmose I is believed to be the first pharaoh to build fortresses. He set up fortresses at strategic points along rivers during the Syria-Palestine campaign. These fortresses gave Egypt its first permanent military presence in the area and protected it from further invasion.

❖ Thutmose I was the first pharaoh to order major construction work on the Temple of Amun at Karnak. He also ordered the building of many monuments and statues.

1510 BCE

1505 BCE

1500 BCE

1510 BCE
Leads a military campaign against Syria

1505 BCE
Conquers Nubia following the region's final revolt

1492 BCE
Dies and is buried in the Valley of the Kings

Weapons

The pharaohs' armies used projectile weapons and hand weapons. Many of the developments in weapons during this period were adapted from Egypt's enemies, who used the weapons against Egypt in battle.

Projectile Weapons

Projectile weapons are objects that can be **propelled** through the air. The main projectile weapon used by soldiers in the pharaohs' armies was the composite bow. It was adopted from the Hyksos, and it was capable of shooting arrows long distances. Other soldiers often used javelins and slings.

Slings were used to shoot rocks and other **ammunition**. Sometimes large slings were used to shoot objects over walls and **ramparts**.

A composite bow was made from horn and wood, and glued together with animal **sinew**. Bronze arrows were used to shoot enemies.

Javelins, or throw sticks, were quick and easy to make. They could be replaced easily if they were lost in combat.

Hand Weapons

Hand weapons are objects that are used in hand-to-hand combat. The scimitar, or *kophesh*, was a curved sword that became the preferred hand weapon for soldiers in the pharaohs' armies. Soldiers also used two types of battleaxes, the traditional piercing ax and the openwork cutting ax. Archers used spears once they had used all their arrows.

Egypians used swords that were as long as 29.5 inches (75 centimeters) and had pointed tips.

The scimitar had a curved blade more than 20 in (50 cm) long and a **hilt** of about 7 in (18 cm) long.

Traditional piercing axes were used to penetrate armor.

A spear was similar to a javelin and was roughly the same height as its owner.

Armor and Chariots

During the New Kingdom, improvements were made to armor and chariots due to developments in materials and design.

Armor

Before the New Kingdom, few soldiers wore body armor. During the New Kingdom, some soldiers in the pharaohs' armies began wearing leather or linen **corselets** that protected their torsos. Pharaohs and nobles often wore leather corselets reinforced with metal scales and decorated with jewels and gold. Soldiers sometimes wore leather or metal helmets into battle, while the pharaoh wore a special decorated helmet.

In battle, soldiers wore corselets and carried shields to protect their bodies.

Shields

Shields were traditionally made from a combination of wood, leather, and **rawhide**, and they usually covered the whole body. During the New Kingdom, bronze shields were introduced. However, these shields were heavier due to the weight of the bronze, and they did not always offer better protection. Sea Peoples who fought for Egypt as mercenaries tended to use smaller round shields, although these were never widely adopted by the pharaohs' armies.

Chariots

Chariots were introduced to Egypt by the Hyksos and, during the New Kingdom, they were adapted to become lighter and faster. Egyptian chariots were manned by two men and sometimes pulled by two horses. The driver, or *kedgen*, held the reins and carried a shield held by a leather strap. The archer, or *senery*, fired arrows using a composite bow. Since the archer needed both hands to use the bow and arrow, the driver protected him with his shield. The archer often used a spear once his arrows had been fired.

Chariots were one of the most important elements in the defense strategy of the pharaohs' armies. They were used at the start of a battle. Chariot drivers charged forward into the enemy while archers released their arrows in an effort to break the enemy lines. Infantry soldiers then attacked the enemy from the front as the chariots surrounded the enemy from the back and the sides and mowed them down with their horses and wheels.

An archer used both hands to fire arrows from a composite bow.

SPOTLIGHT ON
the Battle of Kadesh

─── *Spotlight On* ───

WHAT: The Battle of Kadesh

WHEN: Around 1274 BCE

BETWEEN: Ramses II's armies and the Hittites

OUTCOME: Considered a victory by the pharaohs' armies

The Battle of Kadesh was the largest recorded chariot battle in history. It is one of the few battles that historians have been able to examine from both Egyptian and Hittite sources, and study the battle tactics of the pharaohs' armies. Historians view the battle as a tactical failure for the pharaohs' armies, yet it was considered a victory at the time.

The Strategy

Pharaoh Ramses II's strategy to capture the city of Kadesh could be seen as a failure. Ramses II split his army into four corps, and each corps marched 6.2 miles (10 kilometers) apart. However, the distance between them made it difficult for the corps to support one another. They were split when they crossed the Orontes River at different times. The first and second corps ended up well ahead of the other two corps, who were still on the opposite bank.

The story of the Battle of Kadesh has been carved into this stone wall.

The Turning Point

The turning point came when the first corps, led by Ramses II, captured two men while en route to Kadesh. The prisoners told them that the Hittites had fled in fear of the pharaoh's soldiers. Ramses II believed this story and his corp forged ahead.

Meanwhile, the second corps had been ambushed by one thousand Hittite chariots. These charioteers then chased Ramses II and the first corps away from Kadesh. They ended up more than 12.4 mi (20 km) away from the corps that had remained on the banks of the Orontes River. Ramses II and his corp then fled to a nearby hill and erected a **fortified** camp, where the main Hittite army attacked them. Ramses II sent messengers to the third and fourth corps to stop them from continuing toward Kadesh.

Ramses II fought alongside his men in the bloody Battle of Kadesh.

The Victory

The battle was won when a group of the pharaoh's soldiers arrived by boat during the battle. The Hittites fled for Kadesh, and Ramses II and the remaining corps returned to Egypt. Even though the army had failed to take Kadesh, the Egyptians considered the battle a victory. Scenes from the Battle of Kadesh can found in many temples built by Ramses II.

IN PROFILE: 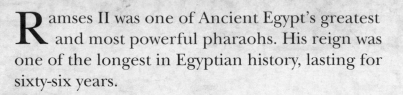Ramses II

In Profile

WHO: Ramses II

ALSO KNOWN AS: Ramses the Great

BORN: 1303 BCE

DIED: 1213 BCE

Ramses II was one of Ancient Egypt's greatest and most powerful pharaohs. His reign was one of the longest in Egyptian history, lasting for sixty-six years.

Under Ramses II's rule, Egypt became more wealthy and powerful than it had been for hundreds of years. He led a number of **expeditions** to regions east of the Mediterranean, and south into Nubia. He also built many great monuments and temples, and founded a new city in the Delta called Per-Ramses.

In 1249 BCE, Ramses II was transformed into a living god at a festival called the Heb Sed.

Notable Moment

Ramses II is believed to have created the world's first peace **treaty**. The treaty was conducted between Ramses II and Hattusili III, the king of the Hittite empire, and it ended years of war between the Hittites and the Egyptians. The treaty was signed in 1280 BCE, after two years of **negotiations**. It was recorded in Egyptian **hieroglyphs** and in the Hittite language of Akkadian.

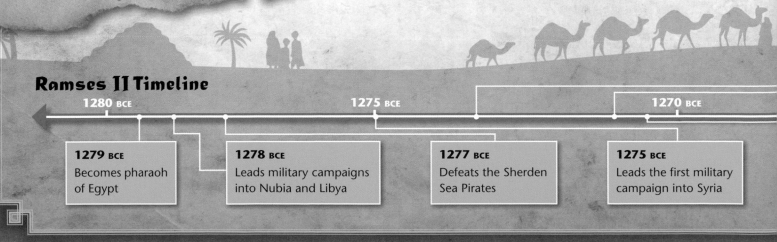

Ramses II Timeline

1280 BCE

1275 BCE

1270 BCE

1279 BCE	**1278 BCE**	**1277 BCE**	**1275 BCE**
Becomes pharaoh of Egypt	Leads military campaigns into Nubia and Libya	Defeats the Sherden Sea Pirates	Leads the first military campaign into Syria

What You Should Know About...

Ramses II

❖ Ramses II was appointed Prince Regent when he was only fourteen years old. This meant that he was the temporary pharaoh in the real pharaoh's absence.

❖ Ramses II was believed to have been in his early twenties when he became pharaoh.

❖ Ramses II was buried in the Valley of the Kings. His body was later moved to a royal cache, which was a place for hiding valuable things. It was discovered there in 1881.

Building Monuments and Temples

Ramses II ordered many monuments and temples to be built during his reign. He extended the great temples of Karnak and Luxor, and ordered the completion of his father's **mortuary temple**. He also ordered the building of a new temple at Abydos, and the building of a large mortuary temple known as the Ramesseum.

1265 BCE	1260 BCE	1255 BCE	1250 BCE

1274 BCE
Leads the second military campaign into Syria and fights in the Battle of Kadesh

1272 BCE
Leads the third military campaign into Syria

1271–1270 BCE
Leads further military campaigns into Syria

1249 BCE
Becomes a living god at the Heb Sed festival

The Role of Religion

Religion was an important part of life for most Egyptians, including those in the pharaohs' armies. The Egyptians practiced polytheism, which means that they worshiped multiple gods. The pharaohs' armies fought wars in order to appease the gods.

The Afterlife

The Egyptians believed in an afterlife, or another journey for the soul. They believed that five different aspects of the self went with a person into the afterlife, including:

- ❖ the heart, or the *ib*
- ❖ the shadow, or the *sheut*
- ❖ the name, or the *ren*
- ❖ the personality, or the *ba*
- ❖ the life force, or the *ka*

The ancient Egyptians carved images of their gods into stone tablets and buildings.

Amun and Re

Two of the oldest Egyptian gods were Amun and Re. Amun and Re later became one god, known as Amun Re. Amun Re was considered the king of the gods, or the most powerful of all Egyptian gods.

Amun

Egyptians believed that Amun was connected to the breath of life and that he gave humans their individual personalities. During the eighteenth dynasty, Amun became a very important god for the pharaohs' armies and temples were built to honor him. Amun was generally shown as a human wearing a horned crown but was sometimes shown with a ram's head and two feathers. These feathers represented the upper and lower parts of Egypt.

Re

Re was connected to the Sun, particularly the midday Sun. Egyptians believed that Re was related to Osiris and that he ruled over the world. It was thought that Re left Osiris in order to rule from the sky, because he was too old to deal with children. All pharaohs were believed to be the children of Re, so therefore they were seen to have a **divine** right to power.

This bronze statue shows Amun as a human wearing a horned crown.

For much of the New Kingdom period, it was believed that Osiris and Isis ruled over Egypt together.

Other Egyptian Gods

There were more than sixty Egyptian gods worshiped during the New Kingdom period, and some of them were more powerful than others.

Osiris and Isis

At the height of his power, Osiris was the ruler of the world, and it was believed that he would one day return to rule on Earth. He was often shown with green skin and holding the **crook** and **flail** that represent divine authority. He also wore a crown and two ostrich feathers to represent Maat, or truth. Isis was the mother goddess who ruled alongside her brother and husband Osiris. She was the mother of Horus and was believed to be more powerful than Re.

Seth

Seth was the god of storms, violence, and chaos. He was often connected to the desert and was shown as one of many animals, including the pig, the donkey, or the hippopotamus. He was the brother and murderer of Osiris.

In the feather-weighing ceremony, Anubis used Maat's feather of truth to weigh hearts in front of the other gods.

Horus and Hathor

Horus was the god of the pharaohs, the ruler of the world, and the god of light. He was shown in many forms, including as a man with the head of a falcon. Horus was the son of Osiris and was believed to protect the world against Seth. Hathor was the goddess of love, beauty, and music, and she was linked to Horus. Hathor was shown as a cow with a sun disk between her horns, and she was often connected to the Queen of Egypt.

Maat, Anubis, and Thoth

Maat was the goddess of truth. She was shown with an ostrich feather, known as the feather of truth, on top of her crown. Anubis was associated with the dead and was often shown as a jackal. He is said to have performed a famous ceremony to determine if a person's heart was honest by weighing it against the feather of truth. Thoth was considered the heart and tongue of Re, and he was the inventor of writing and knowledge. He was believed to record the confessions of the dead, in order to decide who went to the kingdom of Osiris and who was eaten by the dogs of judgment.

Horus was often shown as a man with the head of a falcon.

Army Burials

The **funeral rites** of the pharaohs' armies reflected their belief in the afterlife. Egyptians believed that the *ba* and the *ka* would reconnect with the physical body, or the *khet*, in the afterlife.

Entry into the Afterlife

During the New Kingdom, beliefs changed so that the afterlife was available to everybody who could afford entry, not only to the nobility. This meant that even foot soldiers could pass on to the afterlife.

Elaborate preparations were often made for entry into the afterlife. Egyptians believed that the dead could take possessions with them, so bodies were often buried with valuable possessions. Less wealthy Egyptians may simply have been buried with a bowl and a spoon. The Pharaoh had an elaborate tomb filled with trinkets and valuable objects, such as golden statues. The Pharaoh Tutankhamen was even buried with chariots.

The tomb of Thutmose III was elaborately decorated with hieroglyphs that recorded his achievements in battle.

Preserving the Body

Egyptians preserved the body so that the *ka* could recognize it and return. They also believed that the *ka* ate and drank, so they buried bodies with food and drink.

Mummification

Bodies were preserved through a process known as mummification. Mummification involved removing organs and **embalming** the body. During mummification, the body had a number of spells cast over it to protect it in the afterlife.

Bodies were embalmed with a salty substance called natron, which stopped them from **decomposing**. The organs, except for the heart and brain, were removed and placed in containers called canopic jars. A long, metal hook was inserted up the nostril and into the skull to whisk the brain into a liquid that poured out through the nose. The heart was left untouched because it was seen as the center of all thoughts and emotions.

Egyptians removed a pharaoh's organs and wrapped his body in bandages to preserve it.

WHAT'S IN A NAME?

Osirian Burial

An Osirian burial takes its name from the Egyptian god Osiris. Pharaohs of the New Kingdom received Osirian burials. This involved being mummified, placed in a **sarcophagus**, and buried in a tomb filled with possessions for the afterlife.

The Decline of the Pharaohs' Armies

Toward the end of the twentieth dynasty, the New Kingdom fell into decline. The pharaohs' armies decreased in size and were eventually **disbanded** when the New Kingdom ended.

The Fall of the New Kingdom

The New Kingdom **disintegrated** due to pressures from within and without Egypt. The Sea Peoples took control of parts of the Egyptian Empire in Nubia and Syria–Palestine. Without control of these important regions, Egypt's economy and trade suffered. Egypt's wealthy and powerful priesthood of Amun questioned the pharaohs' power, which put added strain on the empire. In 1070 BCE, the New Kingdom officially ended.

The Fate of the Pharaohs' Armies

The fall of the New Kingdom brought an end to the pharaohs' armies. At the height of the New Kingdom, the pharaohs' armies expanded and became reliant on foreign mercenaries. Eventually, the armies grew so much that the pharaohs could no longer afford to pay the mercenaries. As a result, a number of mercenaries left, and this reduced Egypt's ability to defend itself. Following the fall of the New Kingdom, soldiers continued to fight for Egypt, but the pharaohs' armies no longer existed.

Many ancient Egyptian monuments still stand today, such as the Sphinx and the pyramids.

Glossary

alliance   An agreement between two groups to support each other in times of war.

ammunition   Objects that can be shot from a weapon.

avenged   Inflicted punishment for a wrong.

chaos   Complete disorder.

corselets   Pieces of armor covering the body.

crook   A wooden stick that is bent or curved.

decomposing   Slowly breaking down.

diplomacy   Discussions between countries.

disbanded   Broken up.

disintegrated   Fell apart.

divine   Coming from a god.

elaborate   Rich in detail and complicated in design.

elite   The best or most skilled.

embalming   Preserving a body with chemicals so that it does not decay.

expeditions   Journeys or voyages of discovery.

expulsion   Forcing out.

flail   A wooden tool used to cut grain.

formidable   Inspiring fear and awe due to strength and size.

fortified   Strengthened with walls or mounds.

funeral rites   Ceremonies or rituals performed when a person dies.

hieroglyphs   Ancient Egyptian pictures and symbols used to represent the alphabet and record stories.

hilt   The handle of a weapon or tool.

mercenaries   Professional soldiers hired to serve in an army.

military campaigns   A series of operations to achieve a military goal.

mortuary temple   A temple close to a pharaoh's tomb, built to honor and remember the pharaoh.

negotiations   Discussions between people or groups.

nobility   A rank given to many wealthy and important people in society.

obelisks   Stone pillars with a square or rectangular shaft and a pyramid at their points.

preservation   Protection of an object from damage or destruction.

propelled   Moved forward.

provisions   Stocks of food and other supplies.

ramparts   Defensive walls of castles, built to protect a city.

rawhide   Stiff, untanned leather.

reunited   Brought back together.

sarcophagus   A stone coffin in which Egyptian mummies were placed.

sinew   A tendon or ligament which joins muscle to bone.

social status   The social rank that a person holds in society.

treasuries   The government's funds or wealth.

treaty   An agreement between countries.

Index